How To Treat

ADHD

:

Proven Techniques For Managing ADHD
Symptoms Using CBT

<u>The Purpose Of The Book</u>

The purpose of the book "How To Treat ADHD: Proven Techniques For Managing ADHD Symptoms Using CBT" is to provide individuals living with ADHD, their families, and healthcare professionals with practical and evidence-based strategies for effectively managing ADHD symptoms through Cognitive Behavioral Therapy (CBT). ADHD is a complex neurodevelopmental disorder characterized by symptoms of inattention, hyperactivity, and impulsivity, which can significantly impact various aspects of daily functioning, including academic performance, work productivity, and social relationships. While medication is often a cornerstone of treatment for ADHD, CBT offers complementary approaches that target cognitive and behavioral aspects of the disorder.

Through this book, readers will gain a comprehensive understanding of ADHD and its impact on individuals' lives, including common challenges faced by those with the condition. By exploring the principles and techniques of CBT, readers will learn how to identify maladaptive thought patterns, behaviors, and coping strategies associated with ADHD and develop effective alternatives to promote symptom management and functional improvement. The book aims to empower readers to take an active role in their treatment journey, providing them with the knowledge, skills, and resources needed to navigate the complexities of ADHD with confidence and resilience.

Central to the book's purpose is the integration of evidence-based research and clinical expertise to guide readers in the application of CBT techniques for ADHD management. Drawing from the latest scientific findings and best practices in the field, readers will discover practical strategies for enhancing cognitive flexibility, problem-solving skills, emotional regulation, and impulse control, among other key areas of functioning affected by ADHD. By highlighting the efficacy of CBT in addressing ADHD symptoms and promoting adaptive behaviors, the book aims to inspire hope and optimism for individuals seeking to improve their quality of life despite the challenges posed by ADHD.

Furthermore, the book seeks to address the stigma and misconceptions surrounding ADHD by fostering understanding, empathy, and acceptance of individuals living with the condition. By providing insights into the lived experiences of those with ADHD and offering guidance for family members, educators, and healthcare professionals, the book aims to create a supportive and inclusive environment that promotes awareness, advocacy, and empowerment. Through education, advocacy, and collaboration, the book encourages readers to challenge societal norms and promote equity, accessibility, and inclusivity for individuals with ADHD across diverse settings.

Ultimately, the purpose of "How To Treat ADHD: Proven Techniques For Managing ADHD Symptoms Using CBT" is to equip readers with the tools and knowledge needed to effectively manage ADHD symptoms, improve overall functioning, and enhance quality of life. By fostering a holistic and empowering approach to treatment, the book aims to inspire individuals with ADHD to embrace their strengths, pursue their goals, and thrive in all aspects of their lives, while also encouraging a greater understanding and acceptance of ADHD within society.

Table Of Contents

I. Introduction

- **A. Understanding ADHD: What It Is and How It Affects Individuals**
- **B. The Role of Cognitive Behavioral Therapy (CBT) in Managing ADHD Symptoms**
- **C. Overview of the Book's Approach and Structure**

A. Understanding ADHD: What It Is and How It Affects Individuals

ADHD, or Attention-Deficit/Hyperactivity Disorder, is a neurodevelopmental disorder that affects individuals across the lifespan. It is characterized by persistent patterns of inattention, impulsivity, and hyperactivity that interfere with daily functioning and developmentally appropriate behavior.

Here's a breakdown of how ADHD affects individuals:

Inattention: Individuals with ADHD often struggle to sustain attention and focus, especially on tasks that require sustained mental effort or concentration. They may become easily distracted by external stimuli or internal thoughts, leading to difficulty completing tasks, following instructions, or organizing activities.

Impulsivity: Impulsivity is another hallmark feature of ADHD. Individuals with ADHD may act without considering the consequences, interrupt others during conversations or activities, and have difficulty waiting their turn. Impulsivity can lead to problems in social relationships, academic or occupational settings, and overall self-regulation.

Hyperactivity: While hyperactivity is more prominent in some individuals with ADHD, not everyone with ADHD exhibits hyperactive behavior. Hyperactivity is characterized by excessive physical restlessness, fidgeting, and difficulty remaining seated or engaged in quiet activities. In adults, hyperactivity may manifest as inner restlessness or an inability to relax.

Executive Functioning Impairments: ADHD is associated with deficits in executive functions, which are cognitive processes that enable individuals to plan, organize, prioritize, and regulate behavior. Executive function impairments can impact various aspects of daily life, including time management, decision-making, problem-solving, and goal-directed behavior.

Emotional Dysregulation: Many individuals with ADHD experience difficulties regulating their emotions. They may have intense emotional reactions to situations, struggle with frustration tolerance, and have mood swings or outbursts of anger. Emotional dysregulation can contribute to interpersonal conflicts, stress, and low self-esteem.

Academic and Occupational Challenges: ADHD can significantly impact academic and occupational functioning. Difficulties with attention, organization, and time management may lead to underachievement in school, workplace difficulties, and challenges maintaining employment. Individuals with ADHD may also struggle with completing tasks, meeting deadlines, and staying organized.

Social and Interpersonal Difficulties: ADHD can affect social relationships and interpersonal interactions. Impulsivity, inattention, and hyperactivity may interfere with social skills development, making it challenging to maintain friendships, communicate effectively, and navigate social situations. Social difficulties can contribute to feelings of loneliness, rejection, and social isolation.

It's important to recognize that ADHD is a heterogeneous disorder, meaning that symptoms and severity can vary widely among individuals. Additionally, ADHD often co-occurs with other mental health conditions, such as anxiety disorders, depression, learning disabilities, and substance use disorders.

Early identification and intervention are crucial for managing ADHD symptoms and improving overall functioning and quality of life. Treatment typically involves a multimodal approach that may include medication, behavioral therapy, educational interventions, lifestyle modifications, and support from family, educators, and mental health professionals.

B. The Role of Cognitive Behavioral Therapy (CBT) in Managing ADHD Symptoms

Cognitive Behavioral Therapy (CBT) plays a valuable role in managing ADHD symptoms, particularly in helping individuals develop coping strategies, improve executive functioning skills, and address co-occurring psychological difficulties. Here's how CBT can be beneficial in managing ADHD symptoms:

Cognitive Restructuring: CBT helps individuals with ADHD identify and challenge negative thought patterns and cognitive distortions that contribute to emotional distress and behavioral difficulties. By reframing negative beliefs about oneself and one's abilities, individuals can develop a more adaptive and positive mindset, which can improve self-esteem and motivation.

Behavioral Strategies: CBT teaches individuals practical strategies and skills to manage

ADHD-related behaviors, such as impulsivity, inattention, and hyperactivity. Techniques may include behavioral activation, which involves scheduling and structuring daily activities to improve productivity and time management, as well as implementing behavior modification techniques to reinforce desired behaviors and reduce impulsive or disruptive behaviors.

Organization and Time Management Skills: Many individuals with ADHD struggle with organization and time management. CBT helps individuals develop strategies to improve organizational skills, such as creating schedules, using planners or digital calendars, breaking tasks into smaller, manageable steps, and setting realistic goals. These techniques can help individuals stay focused, prioritize tasks, and meet deadlines more effectively.

Problem-Solving and Decision-Making Skills: CBT teaches individuals with ADHD how to identify problems, generate alternative solutions, and evaluate the consequences of their actions.

By developing problem-solving and decision-making skills, individuals can become more effective in navigating challenges and making informed choices in various domains of life, including academics, work, and relationships.

Emotion Regulation and Stress Management: Many individuals with ADHD experience difficulties regulating their emotions and managing stress. CBT techniques such as relaxation training, mindfulness meditation, and cognitive restructuring can help individuals develop adaptive coping strategies to manage emotional arousal and reduce stress levels. By learning to recognize and cope with emotional triggers, individuals can improve their ability to regulate emotions and maintain emotional stability.

Social Skills Training: CBT can help individuals with ADHD improve social skills and interpersonal relationships. Social skills training focuses on developing effective communication skills, empathy, perspective-taking, and problem-solving abilities. By enhancing social competence and building positive relationships, individuals with ADHD can experience improved social support and a greater sense of belonging.

Family and Parent Training: CBT can involve family therapy or parent training programs to educate parents and family members about ADHD and teach them effective parenting strategies and behavior management techniques. By providing support and guidance to families, CBT helps create a supportive environment that fosters the development of adaptive behaviors and positive family dynamics.

Overall, CBT is a valuable therapeutic approach for managing ADHD symptoms and improving overall functioning and quality of life. It is often used in conjunction with other interventions, such as medication management, educational support, and lifestyle modifications, to provide comprehensive treatment for individuals with ADHD.

C. Overview of the Book's Approach and Structure

The book aims to provide practical strategies and techniques for individuals with ADHD, their families, and mental health professionals to effectively manage ADHD symptoms using Cognitive Behavioral Therapy (CBT). It emphasizes evidence-based approaches and offers a comprehensive guide to understanding ADHD and implementing CBT interventions.

Approach

Introduction to ADHD and CBT: The book begins with an introduction to ADHD, its symptoms, causes, and prevalence. It also introduces the principles and techniques of Cognitive Behavioral Therapy (CBT) and explains how CBT can be applied to manage ADHD symptoms effectively.

Understanding ADHD: This section delves deeper into the nature of ADHD, including its impact on various aspects of life such as academics, work, relationships, and emotional well-being. It explores the neurobiological basis of ADHD and its developmental course across the lifespan.

Assessment and Diagnosis: The book discusses the process of assessing and diagnosing ADHD, including the use of standardized assessment tools, clinical interviews, and collateral information from multiple sources. It highlights the importance of accurate diagnosis for developing targeted treatment plans.

Principles of CBT for ADHD: This section outlines the core principles and techniques of Cognitive Behavioral Therapy (CBT) as applied to ADHD. It explores the role of cognitive restructuring, behavior modification, problem-solving skills, and emotion regulation in managing ADHD symptoms.

CBT Techniques for Managing ADHD Symptoms: The book provides practical, step-by-step guidance on implementing CBT techniques to address specific ADHD symptoms, such as inattention, impulsivity, hyperactivity, organization difficulties, time management challenges, and emotional dysregulation.

Behavioral Strategies and Interventions: This section focuses on behavioral interventions and strategies for promoting positive behavior change in individuals with ADHD. It includes techniques for reinforcement, shaping, token economies, and contingency management.

Coping Skills and Stress Management: The book explores coping skills and stress management techniques to help individuals with ADHD effectively cope with daily stressors, manage emotions, and reduce anxiety. It includes mindfulness practices, relaxation exercises, and cognitive coping strategies.

Family and Parent Training: This section discusses the importance of family involvement in managing ADHD and provides guidance for parents and family members on implementing CBT techniques at home. It includes strategies for improving communication, setting clear expectations, and fostering a supportive family environment.

School and Workplace Accommodations: The book addresses accommodations and support strategies for individuals with ADHD in school and workplace settings. It provides practical tips for advocating for accommodations, collaborating with educators and employers, and fostering a positive learning and work environment.

Long-Term Management and Relapse Prevention: The final section focuses on long-term management of ADHD symptoms and strategies for preventing relapse. It emphasizes the importance of ongoing monitoring, self-management skills, and adaptive coping strategies for maintaining progress and promoting overall well-being.

II. Understanding ADHD

- A. Defining ADHD: Types, Symptoms, and Diagnosis
- B. Impact of ADHD on Daily Functioning and Relationships
- C. Common Challenges Faced by Individuals with ADHD

A. Defining ADHD: Types, Symptoms, and Diagnosis

ADHD, or Attention-Deficit/Hyperactivity Disorder, is a neurodevelopmental disorder characterized by a persistent pattern of inattention and/or hyperactivity-impulsivity that interferes with functioning or development. ADHD is typically diagnosed in childhood, but symptoms can persist into adolescence and adulthood.

Here's an overview of ADHD, including its types, symptoms, and diagnosis:

Types of ADHD:

Predominantly Inattentive Presentation (ADHD-PI): Individuals with this type of ADHD primarily exhibit symptoms of inattention, such as difficulty sustaining attention, organizing tasks, following instructions, and completing assignments. They may appear forgetful and easily distracted.

Predominantly Hyperactive-Impulsive Presentation (ADHD-PH): Individuals with this type of ADHD primarily exhibit symptoms of hyperactivity and impulsivity, such as fidgeting, excessive talking, difficulty waiting their turn, and acting without thinking about consequences.

Combined Presentation (ADHD-C): Individuals with the combined type of ADHD exhibit symptoms of both inattention and hyperactivity-impulsivity.

<h1 style="text-align:center"><u>Symptoms of ADHD:</u></h1>

Inattention Symptoms:

- Difficulty sustaining attention in tasks or play activities

- Easily distracted by extraneous stimuli

- Forgetfulness in daily activities

- Difficulty organizing tasks and activities

- Avoidance or dislike of tasks requiring sustained mental effort

- Frequently losing items necessary for tasks

Hyperactivity Symptoms:

- Fidgeting or squirming in seat

- Difficulty remaining seated in situations where it is expected

- Excessive running or climbing in inappropriate situations

- Difficulty engaging in activities quietly

- "On the go" as if driven by a motor

- Talking excessively

Impulsivity Symptoms:

- Blurting out answers before questions have been completed

- Difficulty awaiting turn in games or group situations

- Interrupting or intruding on others' conversations or activities

- Difficulty following rules or instructions

<u>Diagnosis of ADHD:</u>

Diagnosing ADHD typically involves a comprehensive assessment by a qualified healthcare professional, such as a psychiatrist, psychologist, pediatrician, or neurologist. The diagnostic process may include the following steps:

Clinical Interview: The healthcare professional conducts a thorough interview with the individual and their parents or caregivers to gather information about symptoms, developmental history, family history, and functional impairment.

Behavioral and Symptom Assessment: rating scales, such as the DSM-5 criteria or Vanderbilt Assessment Scales, may be used to assess the presence and severity of ADHD symptoms across different settings (e.g., home, school).

Medical Evaluation: A medical evaluation may be conducted to rule out any underlying medical conditions or factors that could contribute to ADHD-like symptoms.

Collateral Information: Information from other sources, such as teachers, caregivers, or previous medical records, may be obtained to corroborate the reported symptoms and assess their impact on functioning.

Differential Diagnosis: The healthcare professional considers other possible explanations for the symptoms, such as learning disabilities, mood disorders, anxiety disorders, or other neurodevelopmental disorders.

Formal Diagnosis: Based on the assessment findings and adherence to diagnostic criteria outlined in the DSM-5 (Diagnostic and Statistical Manual of Mental Disorders, Fifth

Edition), the healthcare professional makes a formal diagnosis of ADHD and determines the specific presentation type (inattentive, hyperactive-impulsive, combined).

Once a diagnosis is made, appropriate treatment and management strategies can be implemented, which may include medication, behavioral therapy, educational interventions, and support services to address the individual's needs and promote optimal functioning. Ongoing monitoring and support are typically provided to individuals diagnosed with ADHD to track progress and adjust treatment as needed.

B. Impact of ADHD on Daily Functioning and Relationships

ADHD (Attention-Deficit/Hyperactivity Disorder) can have a significant impact on daily functioning and relationships across various domains of life. Here are some ways ADHD can affect individuals:

Daily Functioning:

Time Management and Organization: Individuals with ADHD often struggle with time management and organization. They may have difficulty prioritizing tasks, estimating time accurately, and following through with plans and commitments.

Task Completion and Productivity: ADHD can impair an individual's ability to sustain attention and focus on tasks. As a result, they may have difficulty completing assignments, chores, or work projects in a timely manner, leading to decreased productivity and performance.

Memory and Forgetfulness: Forgetfulness is a common symptom of ADHD. Individuals may have trouble remembering appointments, deadlines, and important details, which can contribute to missed appointments, misplaced items, and other memory-related challenges.

Impulsivity and Risk-Taking Behaviors: Impulsivity is another hallmark feature of ADHD. Individuals may act impulsively without considering the consequences, leading to risky behaviors such as reckless driving, overspending, substance abuse, or engaging in unsafe sexual practices.

Emotional Regulation: Many individuals with ADHD struggle with regulating their emotions. They may experience mood swings, irritability, frustration, and difficulty controlling their temper. Emotional dysregulation can impact relationships and contribute to interpersonal conflicts.

Procrastination and Avoidance Behaviors: ADHD symptoms such as procrastination and avoidance can hinder individuals from initiating tasks or activities that require sustained effort or attention. They may procrastinate on important tasks or avoid challenging situations altogether, which can interfere with goal attainment and personal growth.

Relationships:

Family Relationships: ADHD can strain family relationships due to difficulties with communication, organization, and emotional regulation. Parents may struggle to understand and manage their child's ADHD symptoms, while siblings may feel neglected or resentful of the attention given to the individual with ADHD.

Peer Relationships: Children and adolescents with ADHD may have difficulty making and maintaining friendships. Impulsivity, hyperactivity, and social skills deficits can make it challenging to interact with peers and navigate social situations effectively. Rejection and social isolation are common experiences for individuals with ADHD.

Romantic Relationships: Adults with ADHD may face challenges in romantic relationships due to difficulties with communication, organization, and emotional regulation. Impulsivity and distractibility can contribute to conflicts and misunderstandings, while forgetfulness and inconsistency may erode trust and intimacy.

Work and Academic Relationships: ADHD symptoms can impact relationships in academic and work settings. Individuals may struggle to meet deadlines, follow instructions, and collaborate with peers or colleagues effectively.

Executive function deficits can hinder performance and advancement opportunities.

Self-Esteem and Self-Concept: The challenges associated with ADHD can impact an individual's self-esteem and self-concept. Persistent difficulties in daily functioning and relationships may lead to feelings of inadequacy, frustration, and low self-worth.

It's important to recognize the multifaceted impact of ADHD on daily functioning and relationships and to provide support and accommodations to individuals affected by ADHD. Comprehensive treatment approaches that address ADHD symptoms, enhance coping skills, and promote effective communication and relationship-building strategies can help individuals with ADHD thrive in various aspects of life.

C. Common Challenges Faced by Individuals with ADHD

Individuals with ADHD (Attention-Deficit/Hyperactivity Disorder) often face a variety of challenges that can impact different aspects of their lives. Here are some common challenges experienced by individuals with ADHD:

Inattention: Difficulty sustaining attention and staying focused on tasks, which can lead to incomplete work, missed details, and forgetfulness.

Hyperactivity: Restlessness, excessive movement, and difficulty sitting still for extended periods, which can be disruptive in academic, work, and social settings.

Impulsivity: Acting without thinking about consequences, interrupting others, blurting out responses, and engaging in risky behaviors without considering potential dangers.

Executive Functioning Deficits: Difficulties with executive functions such as organization, planning, time management, prioritization, and impulse control, which can impact academic and occupational performance.

Procrastination: Putting off tasks until the last minute due to difficulty initiating activities, prioritizing tasks, and managing time effectively.

Poor Time Management: Difficulty estimating time accurately, adhering to schedules, and meeting deadlines, which can lead to lateness, missed appointments, and academic or work-related consequences.

Disorganization: Challenges with maintaining order, keeping track of belongings, and organizing tasks and materials, leading to clutter, misplaced items, and difficulty finding necessary items or information.

Forgetfulness: Difficulty remembering appointments, deadlines, instructions, and important details, which can contribute to missed opportunities and incomplete tasks.

Emotional Dysregulation: Mood swings, irritability, frustration, and emotional sensitivity, which can impact relationships and self-esteem.

Social Skills Difficulties: Challenges with social interactions, including reading social cues, maintaining appropriate conversations, taking turns, and understanding social norms, which can lead to social rejection and isolation.

Academic Challenges: Difficulties with concentration, organization, time management, and completing assignments, which can result in academic underachievement and frustration.

Workplace Challenges: Struggles with meeting job requirements, staying focused on tasks, managing time effectively, and navigating interpersonal relationships in the workplace.

Relationship Issues: Difficulty maintaining relationships due to impulsivity, inattention, emotional dysregulation, and social skills deficits, which can lead to misunderstandings, conflicts, and feelings of rejection.

Self-Esteem Issues: Negative self-perception, feelings of inadequacy, and low self-esteem resulting from persistent challenges and setbacks associated with ADHD.

It's important to recognize that the challenges faced by individuals with ADHD can vary widely depending on factors such as age, severity of symptoms, co-occurring conditions, and individual strengths and weaknesses. Providing support, accommodations, and interventions tailored to the specific needs of individuals with ADHD can help them overcome these challenges and achieve success in various aspects of life.

III. Introduction to Cognitive Behavioral Therapy (CBT)

- A. Core Principles of CBT
- B. How CBT Can Be Adapted for ADHD Management
- C. Evidence-Based Research Supporting the Efficacy of CBT for ADHD

A. Core Principles of CBT

Cognitive Behavioral Therapy (CBT) is a widely used and effective therapeutic approach that focuses on the connections between thoughts, feelings, and behaviors. The core principles of CBT encompass several key concepts and techniques that guide the therapeutic process. Here are the core principles of CBT:

Cognitive Restructuring: CBT emphasizes the role of cognitive processes in shaping emotions and behaviors. Cognitive restructuring involves identifying and challenging irrational or unhelpful thoughts and beliefs that contribute to emotional distress and maladaptive behaviors. By replacing negative thoughts with more balanced and realistic ones, individuals can change their emotional responses and behavioral patterns.

Behavioral Activation: Behavioral activation is a core component of CBT that involves engaging in activities and behaviors that promote positive mood and well-being. By increasing participation in rewarding and meaningful activities, individuals can counteract feelings of depression, anxiety, and avoidance.

Functional Analysis: CBT uses functional analysis to understand the relationship between thoughts, emotions, behaviors, and environmental factors. By examining the antecedents and consequences of behaviors, individuals can gain insight into the underlying triggers and motivations for their actions, leading to more adaptive coping strategies.

Skill Building: CBT focuses on teaching individuals practical skills and strategies to manage emotions, cope with stress, and solve problems effectively. These skills may include assertiveness training, relaxation techniques, communication skills, problem-solving skills, and emotion regulation strategies.

Exposure and Response Prevention: In the treatment of anxiety disorders, CBT often incorporates exposure therapy, which involves gradually confronting feared situations or stimuli in a controlled and systematic manner. Exposure therapy helps individuals confront and overcome their fears, reduce avoidance behaviors, and learn that anxiety decreases over time.

Homework Assignments: CBT often includes homework assignments that encourage individuals to practice new skills and apply therapeutic techniques outside of therapy sessions. Homework assignments reinforce learning, promote skill development, and encourage active participation in the therapeutic process.

Collaborative and Empathic Therapeutic Relationship: CBT emphasizes the importance of collaboration and a supportive therapeutic relationship between the therapist and client. Therapists work collaboratively with clients to set goals, develop treatment plans, and identify solutions to problems. Empathy, validation, and nonjudgmental acceptance are central to building trust and rapport with clients.

Focus on the Present: CBT is primarily focused on the present moment and addressing current problems and symptoms. While past experiences and childhood influences may be explored, the emphasis is on identifying and changing patterns of thinking and behavior that contribute to current difficulties.

Goal-Oriented and Time-Limited: CBT is goal-oriented and time-limited, with a focus on achieving specific treatment goals within a defined timeframe. Therapy sessions are structured and focused on addressing targeted problems and developing practical solutions.

Relapse Prevention: CBT emphasizes the importance of relapse prevention strategies to maintain treatment gains over the long term. Individuals learn to identify early warning signs of relapse, develop coping strategies to manage triggers and high-risk situations, and build resilience to future challenges.

Overall, the core principles of CBT provide a structured and evidence-based framework for addressing a wide range of psychological problems and promoting emotional well-being and adaptive functioning. By targeting cognitive distortions, maladaptive behaviors, and underlying patterns of thinking, CBT helps individuals develop more effective coping strategies and achieve lasting improvements in their mental health and quality of life.

B. How CBT Can Be Adapted for ADHD Management

Cognitive Behavioral Therapy (CBT) can be adapted effectively to manage ADHD (Attention-Deficit/Hyperactivity Disorder) symptoms and related difficulties. Here are several ways CBT can be tailored to address the specific needs of individuals with ADHD:

Psychoeducation: Providing education about ADHD, its symptoms, and its impact on daily functioning can help individuals understand their condition and feel empowered to manage their symptoms effectively. Psychoeducation can also help family members and caregivers better support individuals with ADHD.

Skill Building: CBT can focus on teaching specific skills that are particularly relevant to managing ADHD symptoms, such as:

- **Time management:** Learning how to prioritize tasks, estimate time accurately, and use time management tools (e.g., planners, calendars).

- **Organization:** Developing strategies for organizing tasks, materials, and schedules to reduce clutter and improve efficiency.

- **Impulse control:** Practicing techniques to pause and reflect before acting impulsively, such as implementing a "stop and think" strategy.

- **Problem-solving:** Developing problem-solving skills to address challenges related to ADHD symptoms and daily life.

Cognitive Restructuring: CBT helps individuals identify and challenge negative thoughts and beliefs related to ADHD, such as feelings of incompetence or self-blame. By reframing negative thoughts and replacing them with more adaptive beliefs, individuals can improve their self-esteem and coping abilities.

Behavioral Strategies: CBT can incorporate behavioral techniques to address specific ADHD-related behaviors, such as:

- **Reinforcement:** Using positive reinforcement to encourage desired behaviors and reduce undesirable behaviors.

- **Self-monitoring:** Keeping track of behaviors and symptoms to increase awareness and identify patterns.

- **Environmental modifications:** Making changes to the physical environment to minimize distractions and support focus and concentration.

- **Breaking tasks into smaller steps:** Breaking down complex tasks into manageable steps to reduce overwhelm and improve task completion.

Emotion Regulation: CBT can help individuals with ADHD develop skills to regulate emotions and manage stress more effectively. Techniques such as relaxation training, mindfulness meditation, and cognitive restructuring can help individuals cope with emotional dysregulation and reduce anxiety and mood swings.

Executive Functioning Training: CBT can target executive functioning deficits commonly associated with ADHD, including difficulties with planning, organization, initiation, and inhibition. Through targeted interventions, individuals can learn strategies to strengthen executive functioning skills and improve overall self-regulation.

Parent Training and Family Therapy: For children and adolescents with ADHD, involving parents and family members in therapy can be beneficial. Parent training programs and family therapy sessions can provide education, support, and strategies for managing ADHD symptoms at home and improving family dynamics.

Collaborative Approach: CBT for ADHD should involve collaboration between the therapist, individual with ADHD, and relevant stakeholders (e.g., family members, teachers, employers). Collaborative goal-setting and problem-solving can enhance engagement and increase the likelihood of successful treatment outcomes.

By adapting CBT to address the specific challenges associated with ADHD, individuals can develop practical skills, improve self-awareness, and learn effective strategies to manage their symptoms and improve their overall quality of life.

C. Evidence-Based Research Supporting the Efficacy of CBT for ADHD

Cognitive Behavioral Therapy (CBT) has been studied extensively as a treatment approach for ADHD (Attention-Deficit/Hyperactivity Disorder), and there is growing evidence supporting its efficacy. Here are some key findings from research studies that demonstrate the effectiveness of CBT for ADHD:

Meta-Analyses and Systematic Reviews: Several meta-analyses and systematic reviews have been conducted to evaluate the efficacy of CBT for ADHD. These reviews have consistently found that CBT interventions targeting ADHD symptoms can lead to significant improvements in core symptoms, executive functioning, and functional impairment.

Randomized Controlled Trials (RCTs): Numerous RCTs have been conducted to examine the effectiveness of CBT for ADHD across different age groups, including children, adolescents, and adults. These studies have demonstrated that CBT interventions, both individual and group-based, can produce positive outcomes in reducing ADHD symptoms, improving executive functioning, and enhancing psychosocial functioning.

Behavioral Interventions: CBT incorporates behavioral techniques such as reinforcement, self-monitoring, and environmental modifications to address ADHD symptoms and associated difficulties. Research studies have shown that behavioral interventions targeting specific ADHD-related behaviors, such as impulsivity, inattention, and hyperactivity, can lead to significant improvements in behavior management and self-regulation.

Cognitive Interventions: CBT also includes cognitive interventions aimed at modifying maladaptive thought patterns and improving cognitive processes such as attention, working memory, and problem-solving. Studies have found that cognitive restructuring techniques can help individuals with ADHD develop more adaptive coping strategies, reduce negative self-talk, and enhance self-esteem.

Combined Approaches: Some studies have investigated the effectiveness of combining CBT with other treatment modalities, such as medication management or parent training. Combining CBT with pharmacotherapy has been shown to produce synergistic effects, leading to greater improvements in ADHD symptoms and functional outcomes compared to either treatment alone.

Long-Term Effects: Research suggests that the benefits of CBT for ADHD may extend beyond the end of treatment, with some studies reporting sustained improvements in symptoms and functioning over time. Longitudinal studies have demonstrated that individuals who receive CBT for ADHD may continue to experience positive outcomes months or even years after completing treatment.

Generalization of Skills: CBT aims to equip individuals with ADHD with skills and strategies that can be applied across different contexts and settings. Research has shown that individuals who undergo CBT for ADHD are better able to generalize their skills to real-world situations, resulting in improvements in academic performance, social functioning, and quality of life.

Overall, the evidence supporting the efficacy of CBT for ADHD is robust and continues to grow. CBT interventions tailored to the specific needs of individuals with ADHD have been shown to produce meaningful improvements in symptom management, executive functioning, and psychosocial well-being, highlighting the value of CBT as a treatment approach for ADHD across the lifespan.

IV. Cognitive Strategies for Managing ADHD Symptoms

- A. Understanding Cognitive Distortions in ADHD
- B. Cognitive Restructuring Techniques to Address Negative Thought Patterns
- C. Enhancing Cognitive Flexibility and Problem-Solving Skills

A. Understanding Cognitive Distortions in ADHD

Cognitive distortions are patterns of thinking that are inaccurate, biased, or irrational, and they can contribute to emotional distress and maladaptive behaviors. Individuals with ADHD (Attention-Deficit/Hyperactivity Disorder) may be particularly susceptible to cognitive distortions due to difficulties with attention, impulse control, and executive functioning. Here are some common cognitive distortions observed in individuals with ADHD:

All-or-Nothing Thinking: Also known as black-and-white thinking, this distortion involves viewing situations in extreme terms, such as success or failure, with no middle ground. Individuals with ADHD may struggle with this cognitive distortion when evaluating their own performance or accomplishments, leading to feelings of inadequacy or perfectionism.

Overgeneralization: Overgeneralization involves making sweeping conclusions based on limited evidence or isolated incidents. Individuals with ADHD may generalize negative experiences or failures to all aspects of their lives, leading to feelings of hopelessness or self-doubt.

Magnification and Minimization: This distortion involves exaggerating the importance of negative events or minimizing the significance of positive ones. Individuals with ADHD may magnify their mistakes or shortcomings while downplaying their achievements or strengths, leading to distorted perceptions of self-worth.

Catastrophizing: Catastrophizing involves imagining the worst-case scenario or anticipating negative outcomes without evidence to support such beliefs. Individuals with ADHD may catastrophize about future events or challenges, leading to anxiety, avoidance behaviors, and procrastination.

Mind Reading: This distortion involves assuming that one knows what others are thinking or feeling without sufficient evidence. Individuals with ADHD may engage in mind reading by attributing negative intentions or judgments to others, leading to social anxiety and difficulties in interpersonal relationships.

Personalization: Personalization involves taking responsibility for events or circumstances that are beyond one's control. Individuals with ADHD may personalize negative outcomes or experiences, blaming themselves for factors that are outside of their influence, leading to feelings of guilt or shame.

Discounting the Positive: Discounting the positive involves dismissing or minimizing positive experiences, achievements, or feedback. Individuals with ADHD may discount their successes or positive qualities, focusing instead on their perceived failures or shortcomings, leading to low self-esteem and self-confidence.

Emotional Reasoning: Emotional reasoning involves believing that one's emotions reflect objective reality, regardless of evidence to the contrary. Individuals with ADHD may rely on their emotional state as evidence for their beliefs or interpretations, leading to impulsive decision-making and emotional reactivity.

Recognizing and challenging cognitive distortions is an important aspect of cognitive-behavioral therapy (CBT) for ADHD. By identifying and reframing distorted thinking patterns, individuals with ADHD can develop more balanced and adaptive perspectives, improve self-esteem, and reduce emotional distress. Therapeutic interventions aimed at addressing cognitive distortions may include cognitive restructuring, mindfulness techniques, and behavioral experiments to test the accuracy of distorted beliefs.

B. Cognitive Restructuring Techniques to Address Negative Thought Patterns

Cognitive restructuring is a core component of Cognitive Behavioral Therapy (CBT) aimed at helping individuals identify, challenge, and modify negative thought patterns or cognitive distortions. Here are some cognitive restructuring techniques that can be used to address negative thought patterns:

Identify Negative Thoughts: The first step in cognitive restructuring is to become aware of negative thoughts as they occur. Encourage individuals to pay attention to their thoughts and emotions, especially in response to challenging situations or triggers.

Thought Records: Thought records are structured worksheets that help individuals identify, analyze, and challenge negative thoughts. The worksheet typically includes columns for recording the triggering event, identifying automatic thoughts, evaluating evidence for and against the thoughts, and generating more balanced or realistic alternatives.

Reality Testing: Encourage individuals to examine the evidence for and against their negative thoughts. Encourage them to ask themselves questions such as, "What evidence supports this thought? What evidence contradicts it? Is there another way to interpret the situation?"

Examining Assumptions: Help individuals identify any underlying assumptions or beliefs that may be contributing to their negative thoughts. Encourage them to consider whether these assumptions are accurate and whether there might be alternative explanations or perspectives.

Decatastrophizing: If individuals are catastrophizing or imagining the worst-case scenario, help them challenge these catastrophic thoughts by considering more realistic and less extreme possibilities. Encourage them to ask themselves, "What's the worst that could happen? What's the best that could happen? What's most likely to happen?"

Generating Alternative Thoughts: Encourage individuals to generate more balanced and realistic alternative thoughts or interpretations of the situation. Help them consider alternative explanations, more positive outcomes, or different ways of looking at the situation.

Positive Self-Talk: Teach individuals to use positive self-talk to challenge negative thoughts and build self-esteem. Encourage them to replace self-critical or pessimistic thoughts with more compassionate and encouraging statements.

Behavioral Experiments: Encourage individuals to test the accuracy of their negative thoughts through behavioral experiments. This involves gathering evidence by engaging in specific behaviors or actions that challenge the negative belief. For example, if someone believes they are incompetent, they might experiment by setting small, achievable goals and observing their ability to accomplish them.

Mindfulness and Acceptance: Teach mindfulness techniques to help individuals observe their thoughts and emotions without judgment. Mindfulness can help individuals develop greater awareness of their thought patterns and cultivate a sense of acceptance and detachment from negative thoughts.

Practice and Persistence: Cognitive restructuring is a skill that requires practice and persistence. Encourage individuals to continue using cognitive restructuring techniques regularly, even when they encounter setbacks or challenges. Remind them that changing thought patterns takes time and effort but can lead to significant improvements in mood and well-being over time.

By using cognitive restructuring techniques, individuals can learn to challenge and change negative thought patterns, develop more balanced perspectives, and improve their overall emotional well-being. Working with a trained therapist can provide additional support and guidance in using these techniques effectively.

C. Enhancing Cognitive Flexibility and Problem-Solving Skills

Enhancing cognitive flexibility and problem-solving skills is crucial for individuals with ADHD (Attention-Deficit/Hyperactivity Disorder) to effectively manage their symptoms and navigate daily challenges. Here are some strategies and techniques to enhance cognitive flexibility and problem-solving skills:

Cognitive Restructuring: Cognitive restructuring involves identifying and challenging negative thought patterns and replacing them with more balanced and adaptive thoughts. Individuals with ADHD can practice cognitive restructuring by:

- Recognizing negative or distorted thoughts related to ADHD symptoms, challenges, or setbacks.

- Examining the evidence supporting these thoughts and considering alternative explanations or perspectives.

- Generating more realistic and positive interpretations of situations, emphasizing strengths and previous successes.

- Using affirmations and positive self-talk to reinforce adaptive beliefs and build resilience.

Mindfulness Meditation: Mindfulness meditation practices, such as focused breathing, body scans, and mindful awareness of thoughts and emotions, can help individuals with ADHD develop greater cognitive flexibility and emotional regulation skills. By practicing mindfulness regularly, individuals can learn to observe their thoughts and feelings nonjudgmentally, allowing for more flexible responses to stressors and distractions.

Problem-Solving Strategies: Teaching problem-solving skills can help individuals with ADHD approach challenges more effectively. Problem-solving strategies may include:

- Breaking down complex problems into smaller, manageable steps.

- Generating multiple potential solutions without judgment or evaluation.

- Evaluating the pros and cons of each solution and selecting the most practical and feasible option.

- Implementing the chosen solution and monitoring its effectiveness.

- Adjusting the approach as needed based on feedback and outcomes.

Flexibility Exercises: Engaging in activities that promote cognitive flexibility can help individuals with ADHD develop adaptive thinking patterns. Flexibility exercises may include:

- Brain teasers and puzzles that require creative problem-solving and lateral thinking.

- Role-playing scenarios to practice adapting to unexpected situations and considering alternative perspectives.

- Participating in activities that involve shifting attention and multitasking, such as sports, music, or art.

Structured Planning and Organization: Implementing structured planning and organization techniques can support cognitive flexibility and executive functioning skills in individuals with ADHD. Strategies may include:

- Using visual schedules, calendars, and checklists to organize tasks and manage time effectively.

- Breaking down projects or assignments into smaller, actionable steps and setting realistic deadlines for completion.

- Flexibly adjusting plans and priorities based on changing circumstances or unexpected events.

- Reflecting on past experiences and identifying strategies that have been effective in managing ADHD symptoms and improving problem-solving abilities.

Seeking Professional Support: Individuals with ADHD may benefit from working with a therapist or coach who specializes in ADHD management and cognitive-behavioral techniques. A trained professional can provide guidance, support, and feedback as individuals practice cognitive restructuring and problem-solving skills in real-life situations.

By incorporating these strategies into their daily routines and seeking support when needed, individuals with ADHD can enhance their cognitive flexibility, improve problem-solving abilities, and cultivate resilience in the face of challenges.

V. Behavioral Strategies for Managing ADHD Symptoms

- A. Implementing Structure and Routine in Daily Life
- B. Developing Effective Time Management and Organization Skills
- C. Using Behavioral Activation to Increase Motivation and Reduce Procrastination

A. Implementing Structure and Routine in Daily Life

Implementing structure and routine in daily life can be highly beneficial, especially for individuals with ADHD (Attention-Deficit/Hyperactivity Disorder) who may struggle with organization, time management, and impulsivity. Establishing consistent routines and structures can help individuals with ADHD better manage their time, prioritize tasks, and maintain focus. Here are some strategies for implementing structure and routine:

Establish a Consistent Schedule: Create a daily or weekly schedule that includes regular times for waking up, meals, work or school, exercise, relaxation, and bedtime. Consistency in daily routines can help individuals with ADHD develop a sense of predictability and stability.

Use Visual Supports: Visual supports, such as calendars, planners, to-do lists, and visual schedules, can help individuals with ADHD organize their tasks and activities. Use color-coding, symbols, and visual cues to make schedules and reminders more engaging and easier to follow.

Break Tasks into Manageable Steps: Break down larger tasks or projects into smaller, more manageable steps. This can help individuals with ADHD avoid feeling overwhelmed and make progress toward their goals more effectively.

Encourage them to focus on completing one step at a time.

Prioritize Tasks: Help individuals with ADHD prioritize their tasks based on importance and deadlines. Teach them how to identify the most critical tasks and allocate their time and energy accordingly. Use techniques such as the Eisenhower Matrix (urgent vs. important) to prioritize tasks effectively.

Set Clear Goals and Expectations: Establish clear goals and expectations for each day or week. Clearly communicate what needs to be accomplished and any deadlines or milestones that need to be met. Setting achievable goals can help individuals with ADHD stay motivated and focused.

Use Timers and Alarms: Timers and alarms can be valuable tools for individuals with ADHD to help them stay on track and manage their time effectively. Set timers for tasks or activities to help individuals stay focused and avoid getting sidetracked. Use alarms to remind them of important deadlines or transition times.

Create a Dedicated Workspace: Designate a specific area in the home or workplace for studying, working, or engaging in focused activities. Ensure that the workspace is free from distractions and equipped with necessary supplies and materials.

Build in Breaks and Rewards: Allow for regular breaks throughout the day to help individuals with ADHD recharge and maintain focus. Incorporate enjoyable activities or rewards as incentives for completing tasks or reaching milestones.

Review and Reflect: Encourage individuals with ADHD to review their schedules and routines regularly to identify what is working well and what may need adjustment. Reflecting on their progress can help them make necessary changes to improve their efficiency and effectiveness.

Flexibility and Adaptability: While structure and routine are important, it's also essential to recognize the need for flexibility and adaptability. Encourage individuals with ADHD to be flexible in their approach and willing to adjust their routines as needed to accommodate changes or unexpected events.

By implementing structure and routine in daily life, individuals with ADHD can improve their organization, time management, and overall functioning. These strategies can help reduce stress, increase productivity, and promote a sense of control over one's environment. It's important to provide support and encouragement as individuals with ADHD work to establish and maintain effective routines.

B. Developing Effective Time Management and Organization Skills

Developing effective time management and organization skills is crucial for individuals with ADHD (Attention-Deficit/Hyperactivity Disorder) to improve productivity, reduce stress, and achieve their goals. Here are some strategies to help individuals with ADHD develop these essential skills:

Use Visual Tools: Visual tools such as calendars, planners, to-do lists, and wall charts can be highly effective for organizing tasks and managing time. Encourage individuals with ADHD to use these tools to schedule appointments, track deadlines, and prioritize tasks visually.

Break Tasks into Smaller Steps: Breaking down large tasks or projects into smaller, more manageable steps can help individuals with ADHD avoid feeling overwhelmed and improve their ability to focus. Teach them to create action plans outlining each step needed to complete a task.

Set Realistic Goals and Prioritize Tasks: Help individuals with ADHD set realistic goals and prioritize tasks based on importance and deadlines. Encourage them to identify the most critical tasks and allocate their time and energy accordingly.

Use Time Blocking: Time blocking involves allocating specific blocks of time for different activities or tasks throughout the day. Encourage individuals with ADHD to schedule dedicated time blocks for work, study, leisure, exercise, and relaxation to create structure and improve focus.

Set Timers and Alarms: Timers and alarms can help individuals with ADHD stay on track and manage their time effectively. Encourage them to set timers for tasks or activities to help them stay focused and avoid procrastination. Use alarms to remind them of important deadlines or transition times between activities.

Minimize Distractions: Help individuals with ADHD create an environment conducive to concentration by minimizing distractions. Encourage them to identify and eliminate distractions such as clutter, noise, and digital devices during focused work or study sessions.

Develop Routines and Habits: Establishing consistent routines and habits can help individuals with ADHD develop a sense of predictability and structure in their daily lives. Encourage them to create routines for waking up, meals, work or study, exercise, and bedtime to improve consistency and efficiency.

Use Checklists and Reminders: Checklists and reminders can help individuals with ADHD stay organized and remember important tasks and appointments. Encourage them to use checklists to track their progress and remind them of tasks that need to be completed.

Practice Time Management Techniques:
Teach individuals with ADHD time management
techniques such as the Pomodoro Technique
(work for a set period followed by a short
break), the Two-Minute Rule (if a task takes less
than two minutes, do it immediately), and the
ABC prioritization method (prioritize tasks as A,
B, or C based on importance).

Review and Reflect: Encourage individuals
with ADHD to regularly review their schedules
and routines to identify what is working well and
what may need adjustment. Reflecting on their
progress can help them make necessary changes
to improve their time management and
organization skills.

By implementing these strategies and
techniques, individuals with ADHD can develop
effective time management and organization
skills, improve their productivity, and enhance
their overall quality of life. It's important to

provide support and encouragement as they work to establish and maintain these skills.

C. Using Behavioral Activation to Increase Motivation and Reduce Procrastination

Behavioral activation is a therapeutic approach that aims to increase engagement in rewarding activities and reduce avoidance behaviors, including procrastination. It is based on the premise that increasing participation in pleasant and meaningful activities can improve mood, motivation, and overall functioning. Here are some strategies for using behavioral activation to increase motivation and reduce procrastination:

Identify Values and Goals: Help individuals identify their values, interests, and long-term goals. Encourage them to reflect on what is meaningful and important to them in various areas of life, such as work, relationships, hobbies, and self-care.

Set Specific and Achievable Goals: Work with individuals to set specific, achievable goals that align with their values and interests. Break larger goals down into smaller, more manageable steps to make them less overwhelming and easier to approach.

Create a Rewarding Activity List: Collaboratively generate a list of activities that the individual finds enjoyable, rewarding, or fulfilling. Encourage them to include a variety of activities from different domains, such as hobbies, social activities, self-care practices, and meaningful work-related tasks.

Schedule Activities Regularly: Help individuals schedule enjoyable and rewarding activities into their daily or weekly routines. Encourage them to allocate dedicated time blocks for these activities and treat them as non-negotiable appointments.

Use Behavioral Contracts: Consider using behavioral contracts to formalize commitments to engage in specific activities or behaviors. Work with individuals to establish clear goals, expectations, and consequences for adhering to or deviating from the contract.

Practice Behavioral Activation Exercises: Introduce individuals to behavioral activation exercises designed to increase motivation and engagement in activities. These exercises may include behavioral experiments, activity scheduling, behavioral activation diaries, and role-playing scenarios.

Address Barriers and Obstacles: Identify potential barriers or obstacles that may interfere with the individual's ability to engage in rewarding activities. Help them problem-solve and develop strategies to overcome these barriers, such as time management techniques, assertiveness skills, or stress management strategies.

Monitor Progress and Celebrate Achievements: Encourage individuals to track their progress in engaging in rewarding activities and achieving their goals. Celebrate small victories and milestones along the way to reinforce positive behaviors and motivation.

Provide Positive Reinforcement: Offer positive reinforcement and encouragement to individuals as they make progress toward their goals and engage in rewarding activities. Acknowledge their efforts and accomplishments, and provide support and validation when faced with challenges or setbacks.

Adjust and Adapt Strategies: Be flexible and willing to adjust strategies based on individual preferences, needs, and feedback. Collaborate with individuals to identify what strategies are most effective for them and make modifications as needed.

By implementing behavioral activation techniques, individuals can increase motivation, overcome procrastination, and experience greater fulfillment and satisfaction in their daily lives. It's important to provide ongoing support, guidance, and encouragement as individuals work to integrate these strategies into their routines.

VI. Skill Building and Coping Strategies

- A. Improving Emotional Regulation and Impulse Control
- B. Developing Effective Communication Skills
- C. Stress Management Techniques for Coping with ADHD-related Challenges

A. Improving Emotional Regulation and Impulse Control

For people with ADHD (Attention-Deficit/Hyperactivity Disorder), better impulse control and emotional regulation are essential to managing their symptoms and improving their general well-being. The following techniques may aid in enhancing impulse control and emotional regulation:

Mindfulness and Meditation: Meditation, deep breathing techniques, and body scans are examples of mindfulness activities that may assist people with ADHD in being more aware of their thoughts, feelings, and physical sensations. People may learn to monitor their emotions without behaving impulsively and gain more self-control by practicing mindfulness.

Accurately Identify and categorize Emotions: Help people with ADHD learn how to identify and categorize their emotions. Encourage them to use descriptive language to label and identify their emotions so they may better understand their emotional experiences and control their reactions.

Create Coping Strategies: Assist people with ADHD in creating a toolkit of coping mechanisms to control challenging feelings and impulses. These tactics might include cognitive reframing exercises, self-soothing activities, diversion tactics, and relaxation approaches.

Pause and Reflect: Encourage those who suffer from ADHD to stop and think for a minute before acting on impulsive or emotional desires. Urge them to think about the possible repercussions of their choices and assess whether their actions are consistent with their beliefs and objectives.

Use Delayed Gratification: Put longer-term objectives or ideals ahead of instant pleasures or urges to practice delaying gratification. As you wait for the impulse to subside, assist them in identifying ways to divert their attention or find other things to do.

Set Explicit Boundaries and Limits: Clearly define the parameters that apply to impulsive actions and emotional outbursts. Urge people to recognize warning signals and triggers that might precede impulsive behavior and to create plans of action to stop the situation from becoming worse.

Role-playing and Rehearsal: Provide a controlled environment for people to practice reacting to difficult circumstances and controlling intense emotions by using role-playing and rehearsal approaches. Give them advice and comments to assist them come up with more flexible and potent answers.

Stress Management strategies: To help people deal with stress and anxiety more skillfully, teach them stress management strategies including progressive muscle relaxation, guided visualization, and journaling. Promote consistent physical activity, sufficient rest, and wholesome living practices to bolster emotional control.

Social Skills Training: To assist people with ADHD in navigating social settings and interpersonal interactions more skillfully, provide social skills training. Give special attention to developing abilities that might lessen impulsivity and enhance emotional control in social situations, such as active listening, empathy, assertiveness, and dispute resolution.

Seek Professional Support: Assist those who are suffering from ADHD to get in touch with therapists, counselors, or support groups that specialize in helping people with ADHD and associated problems. For the purpose of enhancing emotional regulation and impulse control, cognitive-behavioral therapy (CBT), dialectical behavior therapy (DBT), and mindfulness-based therapies may be very helpful.

By putting these tactics and ideas into practice, people with ADHD may improve their impulse control and emotional regulation, which will improve their self-management, interpersonal interactions, and general functioning. It is crucial to provide continuous assistance, motivation, and affirmation as people strive to enhance and solidify their abilities.

B.   Developing   Effective Communication Skills

Gaining clear expression of oneself, creating wholesome relationships, and amicably settling issues all depend on having good communication abilities. The following techniques may be used to help people become better communicators:

Active Listening: Encourage people to engage in active listening, which is paying close attention to what the other person is saying, seeking clarification when necessary, and giving feedback to show that they understand. To demonstrate that they are paying attention to the discourse, encourage them to keep eye contact, nod, and utilize verbal clues.

Assertiveness Training: Equip people with the skills necessary to properly and confidently communicate their needs, emotions, and opinions. Encourage them to practice utilizing "I" statements to assertively communicate their views and emotions, and teach them how to be forceful without being hostile or passive.

Empathy and Understanding: Encourage people to take into account the opinions, feelings, and experiences of others in order to help them develop empathy and understanding for others. Urge them to show empathy in their interactions, affirm other people's emotions, and recognize their worries.

Nonverbal Communication: Talk about the significance of nonverbal indicators in efficient message delivery, such as body language, tone of voice, and facial expressions. Assist people in being more conscious of their own nonverbal clues and how other people may perceive them.

Clear and Concise Expression: Encourage people to express themselves simply and directly, with language that is easy to understand, in a clear and succinct manner. Before they talk, assist them in gathering their ideas, and steer clear of imprecise or vague terminology that might cause miscommunication.

Active Participation in Conversation: Instruct people on how to take part in discussions in an active manner by asking open-ended questions, showing interest in the experiences of others, and encouraging others to voice their opinions. Urge them to refrain from interjecting and to give others space to talk without interference.

Conflict Resolution Skills: Guide people in identifying the root causes of disputes, helping them to politely and calmly voice their concerns, and helping them to come up with solutions that all parties can agree on. Instruct them in the art of compromise, perspective-taking, and active listening.

Help people develop the skills necessary to provide constructive criticism and affirmation to others in their interactions with them. Encourage them to provide precise, behavior-focused feedback, recognize the contributions and talents of others, and show gratitude and affirmation for the efforts and viewpoints of others.

Feedback and Validation: Talk about the significance of cultural sensitivity and diversity awareness in communication, and assist people in identifying and accepting cultural variations in communication norms, values, and styles. Urge them to adjust their communication style in accordance with cultural variances.

Practice and Role-Playing: Give people the chance to hone their communication abilities via role-playing games, dialogues with others, and hypothetical situations. Give them constructive criticism and support as they develop their self-assurance and communication skills.

People may improve their relationships, become more adept communicators, and handle social situations with more comfort and confidence by adopting these tactics into their everyday interactions. It's critical to provide people constant support and motivation as they strive to become better communicators.

C. Stress Management Techniques for Coping with ADHD-related Challenges

For those with ADHD (Attention-Deficit/Hyperactivity Disorder), stress management is crucial to coping with the condition's problems and maintaining general wellbeing. The following are some stress-reduction methods designed especially for people with ADHD:

Exercise on a Regular Basis: Physical exercise on a regular basis, such as walking, running, swimming, or yoga, may help people with ADHD feel better emotionally, focus better, and concentrate more. Urge them to discover enjoyable physical pursuits and integrate them into their everyday schedule.

Engage in Mindfulness and Meditation: These practices may assist people with ADHD in developing present-moment awareness, lowering anxiety, and enhancing emotional control. To help them relax and reduce stress, encourage them to routinely engage in mindfulness techniques like guided meditation, body scans, and deep breathing.

Establish a Structured Routine: Having a daily routine that is organized may help people with ADHD feel less overwhelmed and have better time management. To offer children a feeling of regularity and consistency, encourage them to set up regular bedtime, mealtimes, work/study schedules, and wake-up hours.

Break Tasks into Manageable Steps: Tasks and Projects may be broken down into smaller, more manageable stages to assist people with ADHD feel less overwhelmed and more in control of their job. Urge them to concentrate on finishing one step at a time and acknowledge each little victory as it happens.

Employ Time Management Techniques: Provide people with ADHD with effective time management techniques, such as making to-do lists, prioritizing chores according to priority and urgency, utilizing calendars and planners, and setting timers and reminders. These methods may assist individuals in maintaining organization, improving time management, and lowering stress associated with obligations and deadlines.

Set Realistic Expectations: Encourage people with ADHD to establish reasonable goals for themselves and refrain from placing excessive pressure on themselves to achieve too much too quickly or to be flawless. Assist them in developing self-acceptance and self-compassion as well as an awareness of their limits and abilities.

Practice Relaxation Techniques: Encourage people with ADHD to use relaxation methods as part of their daily routine. Some examples of these techniques include progressive muscle relaxation, deep breathing exercises, visualization, and relaxing music listening. These methods may ease anxiety, ease tense muscles, and foster a feeling of peace and wellbeing.

Seek Social Support: Advise those suffering from ADHD to look for friends, family, support networks, or mental health specialists for social help. Reduced stress and feelings of loneliness may be achieved by surrounding oneself with a network of people who understand their struggles and can provide support, understanding, and encouragement.

Limit Your Stimulant Intake: People with ADHD may be more susceptible to stimulants like coffee and other drugs, which may make their anxiety and stress symptoms worse. Urge them to cut down on stimulants, which may exacerbate agitation and restlessness, such as coffee, nicotine, and sugary meals and drinks.

Practice Self-Care: Encourage people with ADHD to emphasize self-care practices that support their physical, emotional, and mental well. Examples of these practices include getting enough sleep, maintaining a healthy diet, participating in hobbies and leisure activities, and spending time in the great outdoors.

Individuals with ADHD may enhance their quality of life by adopting these stress management practices into their daily routine and become more adept at managing the obstacles they confront. As they investigate and put these techniques into reality, it's critical to provide assistance and motivation.

VII. Applying CBT Techniques in Various Settings

- A. CBT in School: Strategies for Students and Educators
- B. CBT in the Workplace: Tools for Professionals with ADHD
- C. CBT in Personal Relationships: Enhancing Communication and Understanding

A. CBT in School: Strategies for Students and Educators

Techniques from cognitive behavioral therapy (CBT) may be quite helpful for kids who face a variety of difficulties in the classroom. The following are methods that teachers and students may use to incorporate CBT concepts into the classroom:

<u>**Regarding Students:**</u>

Recognize and Address Negative Thoughts: Instruct kids on how to identify and address negative ideas and thoughts that might be causing them to feel anxious, have poor self-esteem, or struggle academically. Motivate them to replace their negative views with more realistic and balanced ones.

Help Students Develop Coping Skills: Assist students in learning how to cope with stress, anxiety, and other emotional difficulties. To assist students in controlling their emotions and maintaining composure under pressure, include mindfulness exercises, deep breathing exercises, and relaxation methods into your lessons.

Set Realistic Goals: Encourage kids to create attainable and realistic objectives for their academic, social, and personal development. Divide more ambitious objectives into more doable segments, and acknowledge your accomplishments as you go.

Enhance Problem-Solving Ability: Give kids the ability to solve problems in order to successfully handle both academic and interpersonal issues. Urge them to recognize possible solutions, weigh the advantages and disadvantages of each, and put a plan of action into action.

Encourage Self-Advocacy: Give children the tools they need to speak up for themselves and have productive conversations with classmates and instructors. Urge them to voice their worries, seek out the right accommodations or support services, and ask for assistance when necessary.

<u>Regarding Teachers:</u>

Make Your Classroom a Helpful Place: Create a welcoming and inclusive learning atmosphere in the classroom where children experience safety, respect, and worth. Encourage children to collaborate, show empathy, and engage in constructive peer relationships.

Teach Emotional Regulation Skills: Include lessons and exercises that instruct students in identifying and successfully managing their emotions. Give pupils the chance to practice self-calming and relaxation methods in stressful or difficult circumstances.

Incorporate Activities for Cognitive Restructuring: Include activities for cognitive restructuring in class discussions and assignments. Motivate pupils to question harmful thought habits, reinterpret unproductive ideas, and cultivate more flexible self-perceptions.

Provide Social Skills Training: To assist pupils in acquiring efficient problem-solving, communication, and conflict-resolution techniques, provide social skills training. Cooperative learning activities, group conversations, and role-playing games may all be useful teaching methods for social skills in the classroom.

Offer Academic assistance and Feedback: To assist students in achieving academic success, provide them with constructive criticism as well as academic assistance. Throughout the learning process, give clear directions and objectives, break down assignments into manageable tasks, and provide support and encouragement.

Work Together with Mental Health experts: To identify kids who could benefit from CBT therapies and to offer the right support and referrals, collaborate with psychologists, school counselors, and other mental health experts.

By using cognitive behavioral therapy (CBT) techniques in the classroom, children may gain important abilities to better handle stress, control their emotions, and overcome social and academic obstacles. In order for kids to feel empowered to study, develop, and succeed, instructors must provide a caring and supportive learning environment.

B. CBT in the Workplace: Tools for Professionals with ADHD

Cognitive Behavioral Therapy (CBT) can be adapted and applied in various settings, including the workplace, to help professionals with ADHD (Attention-Deficit/Hyperactivity Disorder) improve their productivity, manage symptoms, and enhance their overall well-being. Here are some tools and strategies based on CBT principles that can be beneficial for professionals with ADHD in the workplace:

Time Management Techniques: Teach professionals with ADHD effective time management techniques, such as prioritizing tasks, breaking down projects into smaller steps, and using tools like calendars, planners, and to-do lists to organize and track deadlines.

Goal Setting and Planning: Help individuals with ADHD set clear, achievable goals for their work tasks and projects. Encourage them to create action plans outlining the specific steps needed to accomplish each goal, and provide support in breaking tasks into manageable chunks.

Cognitive Restructuring: Assist professionals with ADHD in identifying and challenging negative thought patterns and self-defeating beliefs that may contribute to feelings of overwhelm, self-doubt, or procrastination. Teach them techniques to reframe negative thoughts and replace them with more positive and realistic ones.

Stress Management Strategies: Teach stress management techniques, such as deep breathing exercises, mindfulness meditation, and relaxation techniques, to help professionals with ADHD cope with work-related stressors and maintain a sense of calm and focus in the workplace.

Problem-Solving Skills: Help individuals with ADHD develop effective problem-solving skills to address challenges and obstacles they encounter in the workplace. Encourage them to identify potential solutions, weigh the pros and cons of each option, and implement strategies to overcome barriers to success.

Organization and Workspace Optimization: Assist professionals with ADHD in organizing their workspaces and developing systems for managing documents, files, and supplies. Encourage them to declutter their physical and digital workspaces, establish routines for filing and organizing information, and use tools like color-coding and labeling to enhance organization.

Work-Life Balance Strategies: Encourage professionals with ADHD to establish boundaries between work and personal life to prevent burnout and maintain overall well-being. Help them prioritize self-care activities, set aside time for relaxation and leisure pursuits, and establish healthy boundaries around work-related commitments.

Communication Skills Training: Provide training in effective communication skills, such as active listening, assertiveness, and conflict resolution, to help professionals with ADHD navigate interpersonal interactions and build positive relationships with colleagues, supervisors, and clients.

Feedback and Accountability: Offer regular feedback and accountability mechanisms to support professionals with ADHD in tracking their progress, identifying areas for improvement, and celebrating achievements. Encourage open communication and provide constructive feedback in a supportive and nonjudgmental manner.

Continued Support and Follow-Up: Maintain ongoing support and follow-up with professionals with ADHD to monitor their progress, address any challenges or concerns that arise, and make adjustments to their strategies and interventions as needed. Encourage a collaborative approach to problem-solving and decision-making to ensure that individuals feel empowered and supported in their efforts to succeed in the workplace.

By implementing these tools and strategies based on CBT principles, professionals with ADHD can develop practical skills, overcome challenges, and thrive in the workplace. It's important to provide a supportive and inclusive environment that values neurodiversity and fosters the professional growth and well-being of all employees.

C. CBT in Personal Relationships: Enhancing Communication and Understanding

In personal relationships, cognitive behavioral therapy (CBT) helps improve understanding, communication, and general dynamics. The following are some methods and techniques for strengthening relationships that are based on CBT principles:

Active Listening: Encourage others to engage in active listening by paying close attention to what the other person is saying without interjecting or planning a retort. To make sure they comprehend and are sympathetic to the speaker's sentiments and viewpoints, teach them to paraphrase what they have heard.

Recognize and Address Adverse Thought Patterns: Assist people in identifying and combating harmful thinking patterns that can be influencing how they see themselves, their partners, or their relationships. Urge them to recognize cognitive distortions or unreasonable views and to recast them in a realistic and balanced manner.

Effective Communication Skills: Give people the assertiveness skills they need to communicate their demands and opinions in an appropriate and transparent manner. Promote the usage of "I" statements to voice issues in a non-judgmental or accusatory manner. Assist them in cultivating an atmosphere of understanding and support by practicing active listening and validation.

Problem-Solving Techniques: Introduce problem-solving strategies to resolve disputes and difficulties in the relationship in a positive way. Invite people to identify the issue, discuss possible solutions, weigh the advantages and disadvantages of each, and then work together to choose a solution that meets the needs of all parties.

Establish Healthy limits: Talk about how crucial it is to establish and maintain healthy limits in interpersonal interactions. Assist people in recognizing and assertively communicating their own limits to their relationships. Promote frank discussion about limits and reciprocal respect for one another's needs and limitations.

Mindfulness and Stress Reduction: Introduce mindfulness techniques to assist people in controlling their emotions, reducing stress, and improving their self-awareness in the context of their relationships. In order to encourage calmness and emotional equilibrium, impart skills like deep breathing, meditation, and grounding exercises.

Conflict Resolution Skills: Give advice on how to resolve conflicts amicably while highlighting the need of preserving empathy and respect in the face of conflict. Urge them to put more effort into coming up with compromises than winning debates or making points.

Relationship Education and Couples Therapy: Take into consideration sending couples to programs that provide relationship education or couples therapy led by licensed educators or therapists. These programs may provide a controlled setting for learning new skills, investigating interpersonal dynamics, and receiving expert advice on particular issues.

Encourage Couples to Honor and Promote pleasant Interactions: Motivate partners to honor and promote pleasant exchanges and intimate times. Assist them in recognizing and appreciating one another's successes, efforts, and abilities in order to create a happy and healthy relationship.

Practice Compassion and Forgiveness: Stress the value of compassion and forgiveness in preserving wholesome relationships. Motivate people to forgive and forget their past wrongdoings, show tolerance for their partners' inadequacies, and handle disagreements with compassion and understanding.

People may improve mutual support, communication, and understanding in their relationships by using these CBT-informed techniques and tools, which will increase their level of personal fulfillment and pleasure. It's critical to provide people constant support and motivation as they manage the intricacies of their relationships and strive to forge closer bonds with their partners.

VIII. Integrating Medication and Therapy

- A. Understanding the Role of Medication in ADHD Treatment
- B. Complementary Use of CBT with Medication
- C. Collaborating with Healthcare Providers for Comprehensive Treatment

A. Understanding the Role of Medication in ADHD Treatment

Especially for moderate to severe instances, medication is often regarded as the first-line strategy in the treatment of ADHD (Attention-Deficit/Hyperactivity Disorder). This is a summary of how drugs are used to treat ADHD:

Symptom Management: Drugs for ADHD assist in reducing impulsivity, hyperactivity, and inattention, which are the main symptoms of the illness. The most often recommended drugs for ADHD are stimulants like methylphenidate (e.g., Ritalin, Concerta) and amphetamine-based drugs (e.g., Adderall, Vyvanse). Moreover, non-stimulant drugs like guanfacine (Intuniv) and atomoxetine (Strattera) are used to treat symptoms.

Neurotransmitter Regulation: Dopamine and norepinephrine levels in the brain are the primary neurotransmitters that are affected by ADHD drugs. These neurotransmitters are essential for controlling executive functioning, concentration, attention, and impulse control—all of which are problematic areas for people with ADHD.

Enhancement of Executive Functioning: Working memory, planning, organization, and prioritizing are among the executive functioning abilities that are often compromised in ADHD patients. Medication may assist. Medication may assist everyday functioning, professional and academic achievement, and daily functioning by boosting these cognitive capacities.

Diminished Impairment and Symptom Severity: Research has shown that ADHD drugs lessen impairment and symptom severity in a number of areas, such as behavior control, social functioning, and academic achievement. Medication for ADHD may help people perform better in many areas of their life by controlling its symptoms.

Enhanced Response to Behavioral treatments in Treatment: Medication may increase the efficacy of behavioral treatments, including parent education programs, academic accommodations, and cognitive-behavioral therapy (CBT). Medication for ADHD symptoms may minimize treatment results by making it easier for the patient to participate in therapy procedures.

Tailored Approach to Treatment: A number of variables, including the severity of symptoms, the type of ADHD, co-occurring disorders, medical background, and responsiveness to treatment, are taken into consideration when choosing an ADHD medication and dose. Healthcare professionals carefully consider these criteria before recommending the right drug and dose for each patient.

Monitoring and Modifications: To guarantee the best possible treatment results and reduce the possibility of adverse effects, routine drug monitoring and modifications are crucial. In order to maximize therapy success, healthcare professionals regularly evaluate the patient's reaction to medicine, including symptom improvement, side effects, and general functioning. If necessary, they will make modifications.

Combined Treatment Approaches: For thorough ADHD treatment, a mix of psychosocial therapies, including behavioral therapy, educational assistance, and lifestyle changes, and medication may be advised. The multifaceted character of ADHD is addressed by combined treatment techniques, which provide comprehensive assistance to those who suffer from the condition.

It's critical to understand that medication for ADHD is a tool for symptom management and functional improvement rather than a cure. The choice to take medicine should be decided jointly by the patient, their family, and medical professionals, taking the patient's preferences, risks, and any advantages into consideration. To meet the various requirements of people with ADHD, medication should also be a part of an all-encompassing treatment strategy that also includes behavioral treatments and support services.

B. Complementary Use of CBT with Medication

One typical and very successful method for treating ADHD (Attention-Deficit/Hyperactivity Disorder) is the combination of Cognitive Behavioral Therapy (CBT) with medication. The following are some ways that CBT and medicine might complement one another:

Taking Care of distinct parts of ADHD: CBT and medication take care of distinct parts of symptoms and issues associated with ADHD. CBT emphasizes on changing maladaptive attitudes, behaviors, and coping mechanisms linked to ADHD, while medication mainly tackles neurobiological aspects underlying the disorder's symptoms. A holistic approach to treating ADHD is provided by the combination of CBT and medication, which addresses both the psychological and neurological elements of the disorder.

Improving Symptom Management: By controlling neurotransmitter levels in the brain, medication may help reduce the main symptoms of ADHD, including impulsivity, hyperactivity, and inattention. By teaching people with ADHD useful skills and techniques to better control their symptoms, cognitive behavioral therapy (CBT) enhances medication. For instance, CBT may assist people in learning organizing skills, enhancing impulse control, managing their time better, and addressing cognitive distortions associated with ADHD.

Improving Executive Functioning: Working memory, attentional control, and cognitive flexibility are examples of executive functioning abilities that may be improved with medication. These abilities are often compromised in people with ADHD. By offering cognitive restructuring methods, problem-solving approaches, and organizational tools to enhance planning, prioritizing, and goal-directed behavior, CBT contributes to the development of executive functioning abilities even further.

Taking Care of Co-occurring disorders: Anxiety, sadness, and social problems are common co-occurring disorders in people with ADHD, and they may call for further support in addition to medication. By focusing on maladaptive ideas, actions, and emotional control techniques, cognitive behavioral therapy (CBT) is successful in treating these co-occurring problems. The combination of CBT and medication may enhance quality of life and general functioning by treating co-occurring disorders and ADHD symptoms.

Reducing need on Medication: Over time, CBT may assist people with ADHD in learning new coping mechanisms and symptom management techniques, which will lessen their need for medication. CBT gives people the tools they need to successfully control their ADHD symptoms and accomplish their objectives without the need for medication by teaching them adaptive ways of thinking and acting.

Long-Term Maintenance of Treatment Gains: Cognitive Behavioral Therapy (CBT) equips people with ADHD with techniques and abilities that they can utilize for the rest of their lives, even if they stop taking their medication. CBT helps patients sustain treatment improvements over time by encouraging long-lasting behavior change and cognitive restructuring, which lowers the risk of symptom return and functional impairment.

Overall, treating ADHD with a combination of CBT and medication provides a thorough and all-encompassing strategy that addresses the disorder's psychosocial and neurological components. Medication for ADHD patients may be used in conjunction with evidence-based psychosocial therapies such as CBT to improve overall quality of life, improve functional results, and better manage symptoms.

C. Collaborating with Healthcare Providers for Comprehensive Treatment

In order to guarantee that patients with ADHD (Attention-Deficit/Hyperactivity Disorder) get thorough therapy, collaboration with healthcare professionals is essential. The following are some essential components of cooperation between patients, their families, and healthcare professionals:

Open and Transparent Communication: Encourage patients and their families to keep lines of communication open and honest with medical professionals about their experiences, worries, and preferred courses of treatment. Good communication guarantees that treatment programs are customized to the requirements and preferences of the person and establishes the groundwork for cooperative decision-making.

Shared Decision-Making: Give patients and their families the tools they need to actively participate in their care by including them in the process of making choices. Weigh the advantages, disadvantages, and personal preferences of various treatment alternatives as you debate them together. These possibilities include medication, psychotherapy, educational initiatives, and lifestyle adjustments.

Coordination of Care: Establish a system for routine monitoring and follow-up with medical professionals to monitor treatment progress, gauge the intensity of symptoms, and handle any issues or problems that may come up over the course of therapy. Plan on having regular check-ins to go over treatment objectives, make any necessary plan adjustments, and guarantee continuity of service.

Care Coordination: Assist in coordinating the patient's care from various medical professionals, such as primary care doctors, psychiatrists, psychologists, therapists, educators, and other experts. To encourage continuity of care and avoid treatment gaps, make sure that information is effectively shared throughout providers.

Holistic Assessment and Treatment Planning: Comprehensive evaluation of the patient's medical history, mental symptoms, cognitive functioning, academic achievement, social functioning, and psychosocial environment should all be part of the holistic assessment and treatment planning process. Create customized treatment programs that take into account the multifaceted nature of ADHD and include a variety of evidence-based therapies suited to the objectives and requirements of the particular patient.

Education and Empowerment: Educate people with ADHD and their families about the neurobiology that underlies the illness, typical symptoms, available treatments, and successful management techniques. Give people the information, tools, and resources they need to speak out for themselves and make well-informed treatment choices so they can take an active role in their own care.

Collaboration in Various places: Encourage cooperation in the individual's family, workplace, school, and community environments, among other places. Develop accommodations, support services, and environmental changes in close collaboration with employers, educators, and other stakeholders to advance performance and well-being in a range of functional areas.

Crisis Management and Emergency Planning: Create crisis management plans and emergency procedures in conjunction with medical professionals to handle mental crises, pharmaceutical side effects, acute symptom exacerbations, and other unanticipated events. Make certain that people and their families are aware of how to get in touch with emergency services and other resources when they need them.

Diversity and Sensitivity to Culture Awareness: Acknowledge and honor the socioeconomic, linguistic, cultural, and ethnic variety of people with ADHD and their families. Treatment strategies should be customized to be inclusive, sensitive to cultural differences, and responsive to the particular values, beliefs, and preferences of various communities.

Constant Quality Improvement: Take part in current projects to improve the efficiency, availability, and cost-effectiveness of ADHD treatment programs. Get input from patients and their families in order to identify areas that need improvement and put into practice evidence-based procedures that support successful results and patient satisfaction.

Collaboration between patients, families, and medical professionals may maximize complete therapy for ADHD, improving functional results, symptom management, and overall quality of life for those who experience the illness.

IX. Overcoming Common Obstacles and Relapse Prevention

- A. Addressing Resistance to Treatment and Stigma Surrounding ADHD
- B. Recognizing Signs of Relapse and Implementing Preventive Strategies
- C. Building a Support Network for Continued Success

A. Addressing Resistance to Treatment and Stigma Surrounding ADHD

A comprehensive strategy that incorporates advocacy, support, education, and destigmatization initiatives is needed to address treatment resistance and the stigma associated with ADHD. The following are some tactics to deal with treatment resistance and lessen the stigma associated with ADHD:

Education and Awareness: Raise people's knowledge and understanding of ADHD among themselves, their families, medical professionals, teachers, employers, and the broader public. Provide accurate information about the neurobiological basis of ADHD, common symptoms, available treatment options, and evidence-based interventions. To promote comprehension and empathy, clear up misunderstandings and debunk myths surrounding ADHD.

Destigmatization Campaigns: Launch destigmatization campaigns and public awareness initiatives to challenge negative stereotypes, misconceptions, and biases associated with ADHD. Tell personal tales of people with ADHD who have overcome obstacles and succeeded in life to show the diversity and power of the ADHD community.

Promote Positive Language: Encourage the use of person-first language and respectful terminology when discussing ADHD to promote dignity, respect, and inclusivity. Steer clear of labels that are disparaging, negative stereotypes, and language that perpetuates stigma and discrimination against people with ADHD.

Peer Support and Advocacy: Facilitate peer support groups, online forums, and advocacy organizations where individuals with ADHD and their families can connect with others who share similar experiences, challenges, and concerns. Provide opportunities for peer mentorship, mutual support, and empowerment to promote resilience and self-advocacy within the ADHD community.

Cultural Sensitivity and Diversity: Acknowledge and honor the socioeconomic, linguistic, ethnic, and cultural diversity of people with ADHD and their families. Make sure that treatment plans and support services are inclusive, culturally aware, and sensitive to the particular needs, values, and preferences of various groups.

Handling Internalized Stigma: Encourage self-acceptance, self-compassion, and positive self-esteem in order to address internalized stigma and self-doubt in people with ADHD. Encourage individuals to embrace their strengths, talents, and unique abilities, recognizing that ADHD is just one aspect of their identity and does not define their worth or potential.

Advocate for Policy Changes: Advocate for policy changes and legislative reforms that promote equity, accessibility, and affordability of ADHD treatment services. Support initiatives to improve access to mental health care, expand insurance coverage for ADHD treatment, and reduce barriers to diagnosis and treatment for marginalized and underserved populations.

Combatting Discrimination: Take proactive measures to combat discrimination, prejudice, and stigma against individuals with ADHD in educational, employment, healthcare, and social settings. Promote inclusive policies, accommodations, and support services that accommodate the diverse needs of individuals with ADHD and protect their rights to equal treatment and opportunities.

Professional Training and Development: Provide training and professional development opportunities for healthcare providers, educators, employers, and community leaders on ADHD awareness, sensitivity, and best practices for supporting individuals with ADHD. Foster collaborative partnerships and interdisciplinary approaches to address the complex needs of individuals with ADHD across different settings.

Encourage Help-Seeking Behavior: Encourage help-seeking behavior and destigmatize seeking mental health support for ADHD symptoms. Normalize seeking evaluation, diagnosis, and treatment for ADHD as a proactive step towards self-care, personal growth, and well-being. Provide information about available resources, support services, and treatment options to empower individuals to take charge of their mental health.

By implementing these strategies, we can work collectively to address resistance to treatment and reduce stigma surrounding ADHD, fostering a more supportive, inclusive, and understanding environment for individuals living with the disorder.

B. Recognizing Signs of Relapse and Implementing Preventive Strategies

Identifying relapse warning signals and putting preventative measures in place are essential components of treating ADHD (Attention-Deficit/Hyperactivity Disorder) and preserving stability and wellbeing. To identify relapse warning indicators and put preventative measures in place, follow these crucial steps:

Recognizing Relapse Warning Signs:

Changes in Symptoms: Keep an eye out for any modifications to or exacerbation of symptoms associated with ADHD, such as trouble focusing, hyperactivity, impulsivity, inattention, and disarray. Keep an eye out for any changes in mood, energy, or general functioning that could point to a relapse.

Impairment in Daily Functioning: Keep an eye out for any changes to your daily schedule, your performance at work or school, your social life, and your self-care routines. Take note of any challenges you are having finishing chores, managing obligations, or staying focused and productive.

Increased Stress and Anxiety: Keep an eye out for any indications of elevated stress, anxiety, or overload since these conditions may worsen ADHD symptoms and lead to relapse. Recognize the environmental pressures and triggers that might cause a relapse, such as deadlines, changes in routine, disagreements, or life events.

Decline in Coping Skills: Pay attention to how adaptive coping techniques and methods for handling ADHD symptoms are changing. Take note of if the person is using maladaptive coping strategies more often to deal with stress and difficulties, such as avoidance, procrastination, impulsivity, or drug abuse.

Social retreat and Isolation: Keep an eye out for indications of social disengagement from once-enjoyed relationships and activities, as well as social retreat. Take note of any challenges the person may be having interacting with others, keeping friendships, or attending social gatherings.

Physical Symptoms: Be aware of any physical signs—such as weariness, restlessness, changes in appetite, sleep difficulties, and psychosomatic complaints—that might coincide with an ADHD relapse. Take note of any changes in your physical health or wellbeing, since these might be signs of underlying dysregulation or stress.

<u>Putting Preventive Measures into Practice:</u>

Preserve Treatment Adherence: Motivate patients to follow their regimen religiously, taking their medications on time, attending psychotherapy sessions, and making lifestyle changes. Assure that you have access to the right medical professionals and support resources to handle any new issues or difficulties.

Frequent Self-Monitoring: Develop self-awareness and self-monitoring abilities to assist people in identifying early indicators of relapse and taking preventative action. Encourage people to use self-monitoring tools, notebooks, or mood trackers to routinely check their symptoms, mood, and functioning.

Stress Management methods: To assist people in efficiently managing stress, anxiety, and overload, teach them coping mechanisms and stress management methods. To lower stress and improve emotional control, encourage the use of deep breathing exercises, mindfulness activities, relaxation methods, and physical activity.

Healthy Lifestyle Habits: Encourage the adoption of healthy lifestyle routines, such as consistent exercise, a well-balanced diet, enough sleep, and thoughtful self-care. Urge people to give priority to pursuits like hobbies, leisure pursuits, and social relationships that enhance resilience and well-being.

Social Support Networks: Encourage people to reach out to friends, family, support groups, or mental health experts when they're experiencing stress or a relapse. Give the ADHD community chances for peer support, social interaction, and affirmation.

Crisis Management Plan: To handle acute symptom exacerbations or mental health crises, create a crisis management plan in coordination with medical professionals and support systems. Determine who to call in an emergency, crisis hotlines, and options to get help quickly.

Flexibility and Adaptability: Encourage adaptation and flexibility in order to help them deal with the stresses and symptoms of ADHD. Assist people in acquiring the problem-solving abilities, resilience, and adaptive techniques necessary to properly handle obstacles and setbacks.

Frequent Review and Modification: Arrange for frequent check-ins and reviews of the treatment plan in order to monitor progress, gauge the efficacy of the program, and make necessary modifications. Work together with support systems and healthcare professionals to meet new needs and improve treatment results.

Through early detection of relapse indicators and the use of preventive techniques, people with ADHD may reduce the severity of relapses, preserve stability, and take proactive measures to control their symptoms and overall health. Establishing a cooperative and encouraging atmosphere is crucial in enabling people to actively participate in their mental health and rehabilitation process.

C. Building a Support Network for Continued Success

Building a support network is essential for individuals with ADHD to maintain continued success and well-being. A robust support network provides encouragement, understanding, practical assistance, and emotional support during times of challenges and triumphs. Here's how to build and nurture a support network for continued success with ADHD:

1. **Identify Key Supporters:**

- **Family Members:** Immediate family members can provide primary support and understanding.

- **Friends:** Close friends who understand ADHD challenges and offer non-judgmental support.

- **Mental Health Professionals:** Therapists, counselors, and psychiatrists who specialize in ADHD treatment can offer guidance and support.

- **Support Groups:** Join local or online support groups specifically for individuals with ADHD and their families to share experiences and receive encouragement.

2. Educate Your Support Network:

- Provide education and information about ADHD to your support network to increase understanding and empathy.

- Share resources, articles, books, and reputable websites about ADHD to help others learn about the condition.

3. Communicate Your Needs:

- Clearly communicate your needs, challenges, and preferences to your support network.

- Express how they can best support you during difficult times and celebrate successes with you.

4. Set Boundaries:

- Establish healthy boundaries with your support network to ensure your needs are respected.

- Clearly communicate your limitations and preferences to avoid burnout and resentment.

5. Foster Positive Relationships:

- Nurture positive relationships within your support network by being present, supportive, and empathetic.

- Show appreciation for their support and reciprocate when possible.

6. Seek Professional Support:

- Consider seeking professional support from therapists, coaches, or counselors who specialize in ADHD.

- They can provide guidance, coping strategies, and tools to manage ADHD symptoms effectively.

7. Join ADHD-Friendly Communities:

- Participate in ADHD-friendly communities, both online and offline, where you can connect with like-minded individuals.

- Attend local support groups, workshops, conferences, or events focused on ADHD.

8. Practice Self-Care:

- Prioritize self-care activities that promote physical, emotional, and mental well-being.

- Set aside time for relaxation, hobbies, exercise, and activities that bring you joy.

9. Be Open to Help:

- Be open to receiving help and support from your network when needed.

- Allow others to assist you with tasks, offer guidance, or lend a listening ear when you're struggling.

10. Celebrate Achievements Together:

- Celebrate achievements, milestones, and successes together with your support network.

- Acknowledge progress, no matter how small, and express gratitude for their role in your journey.

By building a strong support network and fostering positive relationships, individuals with ADHD can navigate challenges more effectively, celebrate successes, and maintain continued success in various aspects of their lives. It's essential to cultivate relationships that offer understanding, validation, and encouragement while providing space for growth and self-acceptance.

X. Case Studies and Real-Life Examples

- A. Illustrative Cases Highlighting Successful Application of CBT Techniques
- B. Insights from Individuals Living with ADHD and Their Journey to Management
- C. Lessons Learned and Key Takea(ways from Case Studies

A. Illustrative Cases Highlighting Successful Application of CBT Techniques

Illustrative cases can provide valuable insight into the successful application of Cognitive Behavioral Therapy (CBT) techniques for individuals with ADHD. Here are two hypothetical cases highlighting the use of CBT techniques:

Case 1: John, a College Student with ADHD

Background: John is a 20-year-old college student diagnosed with ADHD. He struggles with staying organized, managing his time effectively, and maintaining focus on his studies.

CBT Techniques Applied:

Time Management Skills: John works with a CBT therapist to identify time management techniques, such as using a planner, breaking tasks into smaller steps, and setting realistic deadlines. Together, they create a weekly schedule that incorporates dedicated study times and breaks.

Cognitive Restructuring: John learns to challenge negative thoughts and self-defeating beliefs related to his academic abilities. He replaces negative thoughts with more realistic and positive self-talk, such as "I can improve with practice" and "Mistakes are opportunities to learn."

Behavioral Activation: John engages in behavioral activation exercises to increase motivation and reduce procrastination. He sets small, achievable goals for each study session and rewards himself with breaks or enjoyable activities upon completion.

Problem-Solving Skills: John learns problem-solving techniques to address challenges that arise, such as difficulty concentrating in noisy environments or managing distractions. He experiments with different strategies, such as using noise-canceling headphones or studying in a quiet library.

Stress Management Techniques: John practices relaxation techniques, deep breathing exercises, and mindfulness meditation to manage stress and anxiety related to academic demands.

He learns to recognize signs of stress and implement coping strategies to maintain balance.

Outcome: Through consistent application of CBT techniques, John experiences improvements in his time management skills, academic performance, and overall well-being. He feels more confident in his ability to manage his ADHD symptoms and succeed in college.

Case 2: Sarah, a Working Professional with ADHD

Background: Sarah is a 35-year-old working professional diagnosed with ADHD. She struggles with impulsivity, disorganization, and difficulty maintaining focus during work meetings and projects.

CBT Techniques Applied:

Organization and Planning: Sarah works with a CBT therapist to develop organizational strategies, such as creating to-do lists, using digital productivity tools, and breaking projects into manageable tasks. She establishes a structured routine for planning and prioritizing her work.

Attention-Focusing Exercises: Sarah practices attention-focusing exercises, such as mindfulness meditation and sensory grounding techniques, to improve her ability to maintain focus and concentration throughout the workday.

Impulse Control Strategies: Sarah learns impulse control strategies to manage impulsive behaviors, such as interrupting others during meetings or impulsive responding to emails. She practices techniques such as pausing before responding and using self-talk to evaluate the consequences of her actions.

Social Skills Training: Sarah participates in social skills training to improve her communication and interpersonal skills in the workplace. She learns active listening techniques, assertiveness skills, and nonverbal communication strategies to enhance her interactions with colleagues and supervisors.

Stress Reduction Techniques: Sarah implements stress reduction techniques, such as progressive muscle relaxation and deep breathing exercises, to manage work-related stress and prevent burnout. She sets boundaries around work hours and prioritizes self-care activities outside of work.

Outcome: With the support of CBT techniques, Sarah experiences significant improvements in her organizational skills, attentional control, and interpersonal effectiveness at work. She feels more confident in her ability to navigate workplace challenges and communicate effectively with colleagues and supervisors.

These illustrative cases demonstrate the effectiveness of CBT techniques in addressing the diverse needs and challenges faced by individuals with ADHD. By applying CBT principles, individuals can develop practical skills, cognitive strategies, and coping mechanisms to manage their symptoms, improve their functioning, and achieve greater success in various domains of life.

B. Insights from Individuals Living with ADHD and Their Journey to Management

Perspectives from people with ADHD provide important insights on their path to management and coping mechanisms. The following are some frequent observations made by people with ADHD:

1. Recognizing the Neurodevelopmental Nature of ADHD: A lot of people stress how critical it is to recognize ADHD as a neurodevelopmental disorder as opposed to a personal shortcoming or defect. Acknowledging ADHD as a real medical diagnosis lessons feelings of shame and guilt by assisting people in accepting and validating their experiences.

2. Realizing Difficulties and Their Effect on Everyday Life: People who have ADHD often talk about the difficulties they have in their everyday lives, such as in their relationships, jobs, schoolwork, and self-esteem. It may be draining and burdensome to manage symptoms like impulsivity, inattention, and hyperactivity, which can result in emotions of helplessness, worry, and inadequacy.

3. Seeking Medical Attention and Diagnosis: Many people talk about their experiences getting an official diagnosis of ADHD, often after years of experiencing inexplicable problems. Getting a diagnosis may be a crucial step in validating their experiences and providing access to the right care and support networks.

4. Examining Available Therapies: People talk about their experiences trying out various ADHD treatments, such as medication, counseling, lifestyle changes, and complementary therapies. Trial and error, perseverance, and cooperation with healthcare professionals are often necessary in order to determine the best mix of medicines that work for them.

5. Acknowledging Special Skills and Strengths: Many people with ADHD emphasize their special talents and qualities, such as creativity, hyperfocus, and unconventional thinking, despite the difficulties that come with the disorder. Self-acceptance and empowerment may be fostered by embracing these characteristics and redefining ADHD as a source of variety and creativity.

6. Creating Coping Mechanisms: People discuss techniques they use to deal with the symptoms of ADHD and deal with day-to-day difficulties. These techniques include employing visual cues, setting reminders, breaking things down into smaller stages, and engaging in mindfulness exercises. Creating a customized toolkit of coping mechanisms enables people to overcome challenges and reach their full potential.

7. Establishing Networks of Support: For those with ADHD, creating a network of friends, family, peers, and experts who can assist them is essential. Improving quality of life and controlling ADHD may be greatly aided by having sympathetic, understanding people in one's life who provide support, validation, and helpful advice.

8. Promoting Advocacy and Self-Awareness: A lot of people emphasize how crucial self-awareness and self-advocacy are to successfully treating ADHD. People may take an active part in their treatment and seek well-being-promoting techniques by learning about ADHD, recognizing their own strengths and problems, and speaking up for their needs.

9. Accepting Development and Adaptability: People with ADHD often exhibit amazing resilience, adaptation, and tenacity in their road to management, despite the challenges they experience. A growth attitude, learning from failures, and acknowledging and appreciating little victories are all vital components of the process.

10. Offering Support and Sharing Experiences: Making connections with others who have experienced similar things as them while living with ADHD may provide comfort and validation for many people. People with ADHD develop a feeling of community and belonging via exchanging personal tales, lending support, and picking up tips and tricks from one another.

People who are living with ADHD help to raise awareness, understanding, and acceptance of the illness by sharing their perspectives and experiences. Their experiences provide others courage, resiliency, and hope, enabling them to face their own path to management with compassion and assurance.

C. Lessons Learned and Key Takeaways from Case Studies

Lessons learned and key takeaways from case studies involving individuals with ADHD and their treatment journey offer valuable insights into effective management strategies and best practices. Here are some lessons learned and key takeaways based on the case studies provided:

1. Individualized Treatment Approach:

- **Lesson Learned:** Each individual with ADHD has unique strengths, challenges, and treatment needs that require a personalized approach.

- **Key Takeaway:** Tailoring treatment plans to address the specific symptoms, preferences, and goals of the individual maximizes effectiveness and promotes engagement in treatment.

2. Holistic Treatment Planning:

- **Lesson Learned:** Effective management of ADHD often involves a combination of pharmacological, psychotherapeutic, educational, and lifestyle interventions.

- **Key Takeaway:** Integrating multiple treatment modalities in a comprehensive and coordinated manner addresses the multidimensional nature of ADHD and promotes holistic well-being.

3. Collaboration and Communication:

- **Lesson Learned:** Collaboration among individuals, families, healthcare providers, educators, and support networks is essential for optimizing treatment outcomes and supporting the individual with ADHD.

- **Key Takeaway:** Establishing open, transparent, and respectful communication channels fosters collaboration, shared decision-making, and continuity of care across different settings.

4. Strength-Based Approach:

- **Lesson Learned:** Recognizing and harnessing the unique strengths and abilities of individuals with ADHD promotes self-esteem, resilience, and empowerment.

- **Key Takeaway:** Emphasizing strengths-based interventions and reframing challenges as opportunities for growth and development enhances self-confidence and motivation for positive change.

5. Building Coping Skills:

- **Lesson Learned:** Equipping individuals with ADHD with practical coping skills and strategies empowers them to manage symptoms, navigate challenges, and achieve greater independence.

- **Key Takeaway:** Teaching problem-solving skills, emotion regulation techniques, organization strategies, and stress management tools strengthens adaptive coping mechanisms and enhances resilience.

6. Addressing Co-occurring Conditions:

- **Lesson Learned:** Many individuals with ADHD experience co-occurring conditions, such as anxiety, depression, learning disabilities, or executive function deficits, which require targeted interventions.

- **Key Takeaway:** Identifying and addressing co-occurring conditions through integrated treatment approaches improves overall functioning, reduces symptom burden, and enhances quality of life.

7. Celebrating Progress and Successes:

- **Lesson Learned:** Recognizing and celebrating incremental progress, achievements, and milestones along the treatment journey fosters motivation, self-efficacy, and positive reinforcement.

- **Key Takeaway:** Acknowledging successes, no matter how small, boosts self-confidence, reinforces adaptive behaviors, and sustains momentum for continued growth and improvement.

8. Continuity of Care and Follow-Up:

- **Lesson Learned:** Ongoing monitoring, evaluation, and adjustment of treatment plans are essential for maintaining treatment gains, preventing relapse, and addressing evolving needs.

- **Key Takeaway:** Establishing regular follow-up appointments, check-ins, and review sessions with healthcare providers promotes accountability, tracks progress, and ensures responsiveness to changing circumstances.

By synthesizing lessons learned and key takeaways from case studies, individuals, families, healthcare providers, educators, and support networks can collaborate more effectively in developing tailored, evidence-based interventions that optimize outcomes and promote flourishing in individuals with ADHD.

XI. Conclusion

- A. Recap of Key Concepts and Strategies Discussed Throughout the Book
- B. Encouragement for Continued Growth and Improvement in Managing ADHD

A. Recap of Key Concepts and Strategies Discussed Throughout the Book

Comprehending ADHD: Acquiring knowledge regarding the disorder's signs, origins, neurology, and effects on day-to-day activities is crucial for successful handling.

Diagnosis and Assessment: In order to diagnose ADHD and rule out other potential disorders, it is imperative that you have a comprehensive assessment and diagnosis from licensed healthcare specialists.

Multimodal Treatment Approach: Understanding that a multimodal strategy to treating ADHD is often necessary, including medication, counseling, behavioral therapies, lifestyle changes, and accommodations for school.

Medicine Management: This section explains the role that medicine plays in controlling the symptoms of ADHD. It covers stimulant and non-stimulant drugs, their modes of action, possible adverse effects, and how to check their efficacy.

Cognitive behavioral therapy (CBT): Applying CBT methods to regulate emotions and behaviors linked to ADHD, correct cognitive distortions, build coping mechanisms, boost executive functioning, and improve problem-solving skills.

Organization and Time Management: Putting organizational techniques into practice to prioritize activities, cut down on procrastination, and enhance time management. These techniques include utilizing task lists, calendars, planners, and reminders.

Social Skills Training: Gaining knowledge in assertiveness, communication, and dispute resolution tactics can help you navigate social situations, strengthen peer connections, and improve interpersonal relationships.

Stress Management and Self-Care: To manage stress, enhance wellbeing, and avoid burnout, practice mindfulness, relaxation methods, physical activity, enough sleep, and good living practices.

Educational boost and Accommodations: To address learning obstacles, boost academic performance, and encourage self-advocacy, individuals may use educational support services, accommodations, and resources in academic contexts.

Creating a Support System: Putting together a network of mentors, peers, family, friends, medical professionals, and community resources to provide support, understanding, and hands-on help in managing ADHD.

Self-Awareness and Advocacy: Acquiring the knowledge, abilities, and optimistic outlook necessary to accept one's abilities and shortcomings, make reasonable objectives, and actively participate in one's own care and welfare.

Continued Learning and development: Understanding that dealing with ADHD is a lifelong process that calls for constant learning, adaptability, development, and resilience; it also means being willing to try out novel approaches and ask for help when necessary.

These fundamental ideas and techniques provide the basis for good ADHD management and enhance the quality of life for those who are affected by the disorder. They stress the need for a comprehensive and individualized approach to therapy that takes into account the various needs and assets of people with ADHD.

B. Encouragement for Continued Growth and Improvement in Managing ADHD

Supporting ongoing development and enhancement in the management of ADHD is crucial for people navigating the intricacies of the disorder. Here are some inspiring words:

Honor Your Progress, No Matter How Little: Acknowledge and commemorate each accomplishment as you progress toward managing ADHD. Whether it's finishing a task, trying a new coping mechanism, or asking for help, every success matters and should be celebrated.

Accept Your Special Skills and Strengths: Keep in mind that your personality is more complex than your ADHD. Accept the qualities, skills, and distinct viewpoints that make you who you are. Your enthusiasm, vigor, and inventiveness can be great assets in both your personal and professional lives.

Be Patient and Kind to Yourself: Managing ADHD is a journey with ups and downs, so be patient and kind to yourself. Be gentle and patient with yourself as you overcome obstacles and disappointments along the path. Be kind and understanding to yourself as you would a friend going through a similar ordeal.

Focus on What You Can Control: While some aspects of ADHD may feel overwhelming or frustrating, it's important to keep your attention on the things that you can control. Take proactive efforts to control your symptoms, seek help when required, and speak for your needs and preferences.

Stay Connected and Seek Support: Remember that you are not alone in your journey. Stay connected with helpful friends, family members, healthcare practitioners, and community services that may give encouragement, direction, and validation. Sharing experiences and thoughts with those who understand may be immensely powerful.

Practice Self-Care Regularly: Prioritize self-care habits that feed your body, mind, and soul. Make time for things that offer you pleasure, relaxation, and contentment, whether it's spending time outdoors, indulging in creative hobbies, or practicing mindfulness and meditation.

Keep Learning and Growing: Stay interested and open to learning new ideas, approaches, and insights for controlling ADHD. Educate yourself on the latest research, treatment choices, and self-help tools that may assist your road to health.

Set Realistic Goals and Expectations: Set realistic goals and expectations for yourself, taking into consideration your specific abilities, problems, and circumstances. Break huge objectives into smaller, realistic stages, and celebrate your accomplishments along the way.

Celebrate Your Resilience and Perseverance: Recognize the tenacity and persistence you display every day in managing ADHD. Each time you tackle a difficulty head-on, adjust to change, or overcome hurdles, you are developing resilience and enhancing your capacity to flourish.

Believe in Your Potential for Growth and Success: Above all, believe in your potential for growth and success, despite the hurdles you may confront. You are competent, resourceful, and resilient, and you have the capacity to build a life filled with purpose, satisfaction, and meaning.

By accepting these words of encouragement and keeping dedicated to your path of development and progress, you may continue to manage ADHD efficiently and live a satisfying and meaningful life. Never forget that every step you take, no matter how little, puts you one step closer to your dreams and ambitions.